WALK
AROUND

by stepro books

WALK
AROUND

"A photograph is a secret about a secret. The more it tells you the less you know."
— **Diane Arbus**

NO DURIANS
FINE 2,000 BAHT

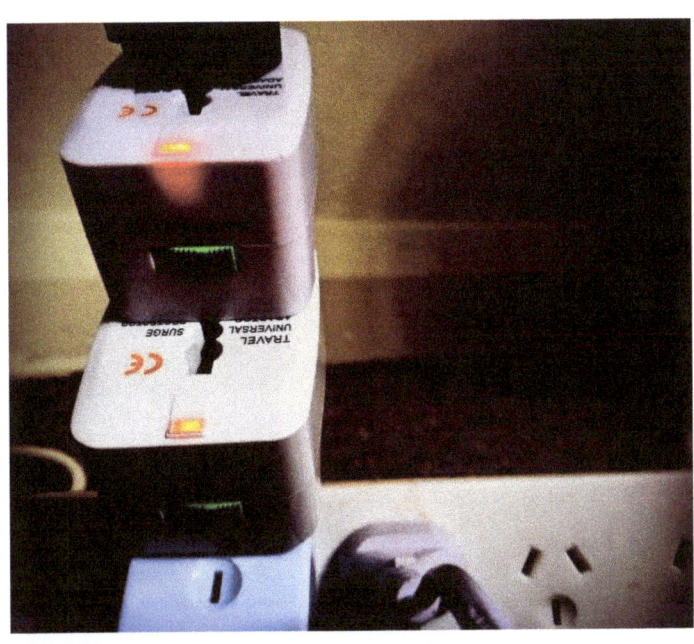

THE HARBOUR IS AN IRONING BOARD.
FLAT IRON TUGS DASH SMOOTHING TOWARD
ANY SHIRT OF A SHIP, ANY PILLOWSLIP
OF A FREIGHTER THEY'D CREASE
MUST BE IRONED FLAT AS WASHING FROM THE SEA.

Chimney Cakes

raditional Hungarian Freshly Baked Pastry & Fried Brea

Cinnamon Hazelnut Almond Walnut Cocoa Plum   Plain (Salty Garlic)   Sour Cream   Cheese   Cheese, Sour Cream   Chee
                                                    with Kransky   and Kransky   and Kransky   and Kransky   Sprir
                                                                                                                                               and

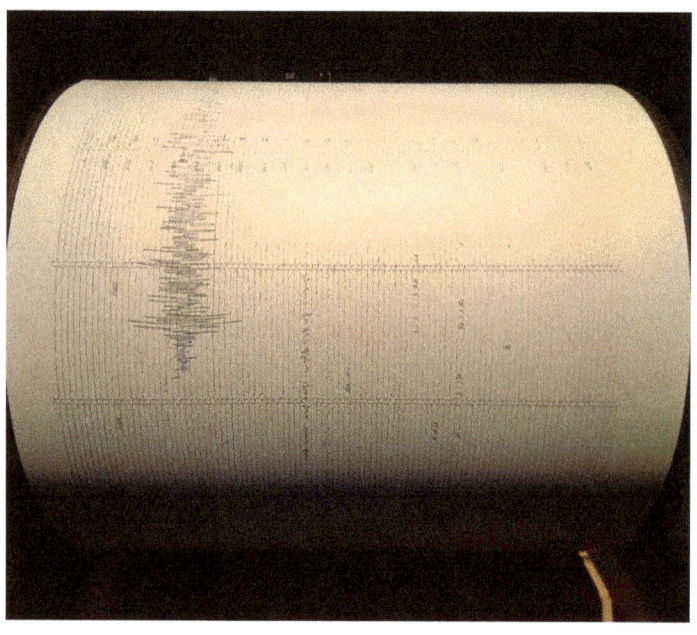

CPSIA information can be obtained
at www.ICGtesting.com
Printed in the USA
BVHW051011020919
557346BV00021B/2631/P